The Magic Book

Jane Bull

A Dorling Kindersley Book

LONDON, NEW YORK, MUNICH, PARIS,
MELBOURNE, DELHI

DESIGN • Jane Bull
TEXT • Penelope York
PHOTOGRAPHY • Andy Crawford
DESIGN ASSISTANCE • Laura Roberts

MANAGING ART EDITOR • Rachael Foster
PUBLISHING MANAGER • Mary Ling
PRODUCTION • Melanie Dowland
DTP DESIGNER • Almudena Díaz

For Charlotte, Billy, and James

First published in Great Britain in 2002 by
Dorling Kindersley Limited
80 Strand,
London WC2R 0RL

A Penguin Company

2 4 6 8 10 9 7 5 3 1

A CIP catalogue record for this book
is available from the British Library

ISBN: 0-7513-3949-0

Colour reproduction by GRB Editrice S.r.l., Verona, Italy
Printed and bound in Italy by L.E.G.O.

See our complete
catalogue at
www.dk.com

Magic tricks before your eyes

Within this Book of Magic

To read this book . . .

Hey Presto! 4-5

Bag of Tricks 6-7

How to Make your Bewitched Bag 8-9

Baffling Balloons 10-11

How to Prepare the Baffling Balloons 12-13

Floating Wands 14-15

. . . weave a magic spell . . .

The Disappearing Handkerchief 16-17

How to Make the Hankie Disappear 18-19

The Vanishing Coin 20-21

Magic Wallet 22-23

How to Make the Magic Wallet 24-25

Miracle Butterflies 26-27

Bewildering Boxes! 28-31

. . . and open sesame!

Mind Power 32-33

Mind-Reading Miracles 34-35

Mathemagic 36-37

Hissing Spells and Powerful Potions 38-39

What Makes a Powerful Potion? 40-42

The Magic Book 43

Quick Tricks 44-47

Index 48

Hey Presto!

Putting on a good show is one of the most important parts of being a true magician or wizard. Take the centre stage and entertain, astonish, and mystify. It's all up to you and a little magic!

From this magic bag right here a fluffy rabbit will appear!

ta daaa

Practise, Practise

The first and most important rule about performing magic is to practise. You need to make sure that all the audience sees is an astonishing trick – not the way you do it. Practise in front of a mirror until you are absolutely perfect. Work out all your movements carefully.

Practice makes perfect

Planning the Show

Before the show, plan exactly the order in which you are going to do the tricks and be prepared. Work out your speeches and keep talking to the audience as this will take their minds off working out how you do the trick.

Polish up your act

⭐ Follow the Magician's Code

✳ Never give away any of your magical secrets. Once the secret is out, it's gone forever.

✳ Prepare your tricks beforehand – the slicker you are, the better – Keep practising.

✳ **Never repeat a trick** - You are bound to give the secret away.

Preparing the Props

Every good magician knows that you need a hidden area on your stage for quick retrieval and storage. Take two cardboard boxes and place one on top of the other. Drape a piece of cloth over the top, then a decorated paper napkin over the surface. There you have it, a concealed compartment! Make sure your audience NEVER sees what's inside.

Conjure up a spectacular show!

A Little Drama

Magic shows are strange and exciting events, so add a little mystery and drama to your performance. Dress the part and give it everything you've got! Use flourishing movements and exaggerate the magic words you use – try inventing some spells to chant.

Bag of Tricks

This bag is not what it seems – it has the power to transform anything that enters it.

In go some handkerchiefs one by one...

Abracadabra!

Hey Presto!
Out they come...

...all knotted

8

What goes in doesn't always come out...

That's magic!

Quick, hide your valuables or they'll disappear!

How to Make your Bewitched Bag

Grab the limelight using the amazing enchanted bag. All you need is the bag, two sets of identical, brightly-coloured handkerchiefs, and lots of practice.

Glue together three pieces of fabric, about 25 x 20 cm (10 x 8 in) in size, leaving the top open.

Glue the material

Sew the three sides together to strengthen the bag.

Sew up the edges

Decorate the front

What's the Bag's Secret?

Secret pocket

Front pocket

This clever bag is actually not just one bag but two. It has two pockets, so that you can put the single handkerchiefs in one part while the knotted ones will already be in the other part ready for you to produce at the end.

Preparing your Trick

Knot together one set of handkerchiefs and place them in a pocket. Then fold down the top of the bag so that the empty pocket is open for the audience to feel inside it. Practise folding down the top — you will see that you can expose the pocket one at a time. When you have mastered it try putting other things into the bag as well.

In go three shiny cars ...out they come on the socks!

8

Performing the Trick

Explain to the audience that you have an empty bag. Let them see and feel inside it. Yes, it's empty. Now, with a dramatic flourish, put the handerkerchiefs into the bag one at a time.

Fold over the top, revealing the empty pocket

1 I'm putting the hankies in one by one

2 Now I turn up the sides of the bag

3 Abracadabra!

4 I fold over the top of the bag to reveal the secret pocket

5 Swishhh! Wow! A trail of tissues, all tied up

9

Baffling Balloons

It's impossible, it can't be done!

Bang!

or rather no bang! However much you pierce them, they simply won't pop!

☆ Keep your cool,
pull out the sticks
with style

No bang?
No pop?

Wow! They go
through the balloon!

How to Prepare the Baffling Balloons

Don't inflate the balloon too much.

Non-Pop Balloon

All you need for this amazing trick is some sticky tape. Simply stick a piece on the balloon and, miraculously, you can poke your sharp sticks through – yes, it really works! Choose some sticks with the sharpest points – or a pin will do instead. Prepare your balloon with tape before you show the audience.

Stick on a strip of tape about 2 cm (1/2 in) long.

Clear sticky tape

Very sharp point

Long cocktail sticks

Be bold, stick it through!

Will it go POP?

Can you stand the suspense?

Skewered Balloon

The secret of this trick is to prepare the balloon very carefully before you show anyone. Once all of the skewer are in place you won't fail to amaze. Practise removing the balloon from the tube, for the end of the trick, without showing that it is twisted.

You will need a cardboard tube, such as an old food container.

This tube is 13 x 8 cm (5 x 3 in)

Poke some holes through the roll – look at the box on the top right to see where you should make them.

Ask an adult ... to make the holes with something sharp.

Paint the tube silver, to make it look like metal, and decorate it.

Add some decorati...

Blow up a long balloon, but not too much or you will not be able to twist it.

Blow up the balloon

Pull the roll carefully onto the balloon.

Twist the balloon in the middle and cover the twist with the roll.

Give it a twist and slip on the tube

Push the sticks through, avoiding the twisted centre.

You may have to push back the balloon with your thumb to help get the sticks through.

What? No pop?

Let me share the secret

I twist the balloon in the middle to keep it from being skewered. But don't tell anyone!

Don't pull the sticks out too fast or the balloon may pop.

Look carefully to see how the skewers miss the centre of the roll, which is where the balloon twist goes.

Performing the Trick

✴ Set up the balloon with the sticks before you start your baffling performance.

✴ Expect ooohs and aaahs as the audience inspects it.

✴ Pull the skewers out slowly, one at a time.

✴ But it is still blown up!

Finally
secretly untwist and remove the balloon.

Floating Wands

As if by magic the wand floats up and down through the air. But no-one is touching it, so how does it work?

As the magician pulls the string...

...up and down goes the magic wand

1 Take a cardboard tube

Choose a tube abou[t] 30 cm long and 4 c[m] across (12 in x 1½ [in])

2 Prepare the secret inside

 Paper-clip

 Undo the clip and make a loop at one end.

Fix the clip

Make a hole at the end of the tube.

Push the clip through the hole.

Bend the clip around the outside of the tube.

Tape the clip in place.

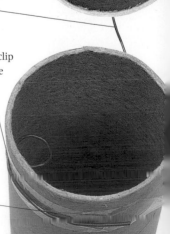

3 If you could see inside

Cut two pieces of string 50 cm (20 in) long.

String 2
Knot one end to a paper-clip and thread string 1 through the clip. Thread string 2 through the top of the tube.

String 1
Attach it, by tying a knot, to the loop inside the tube.

4 Now try it out

Pull up string number 2. It's magic! The wand goes up.

Let the string go down and the wand goes down.

Your tube will not be see-through, of course. This clear tube is to demonstrate how it works.

Don't give away the levitating wand's secret

Pull this string to make the wand go up. Let it go and the wand will move down.

Decorate your finished wand

Wrap the tube up in brightly-coloured paper and decorate it.

Wand Act

Hold the wand up to your audience, while holding both pieces of string, to show them that it's quite normal. Gradually pull the top string while holding the bottom one tightly to make it move up and down. Listen to the gasps from the audience – it's sensational!

Hold this end of the string steady, the other string will do the work.

The Disappearing Handkerchief

It's extraordinary! How is it done? You can't make a handkerchief disappear. Oh yes you can – and it's really very simple. All you need is a silk hankie and a few magic words!

I'm going to make it disappear before your very eyes

1

Bring it back

Blow on your fist

4

Hocus Pocus handkerchief disappear

2

Whoosh! It's gone!

3

Watch carefully here it comes...

5

...Ta daaa the handkerchief has come back

What an illusion!

6

17

How to Make the Hankie Disappear

The big secret to this simple trick is what is known, in the wizard world, as a thumb tip. You may find one in a local magic shop. Otherwise you can make your own. It is a very useful prop for future conjuring tricks.

A thumb tip does the trick

Make sure the hankie and your thumb can fit inside!

Try a plaster instead of paint

Making your Thumb Tip

✶ Measure a strip of card around your thumb and tape it up into a cylinder shape – it should slide on and off your thumb easily.

✶ Tape another strip of card over one end.

✶ Glue some kitchen towel all around the card shape to smooth it out, then paint it with a skin-coloured paint or cover it with a plaster.

✶ Draw on a nail and a knuckle.

18

The Trick

The way to master this trick is simply to practise. Follow the steps to find out how to perform it, then try it in front of the mirror so that you can see what the audience sees. Try using a silk handkerchief as it will squash into a tiny ball and fit into your thumb tip better. Use dramatic movements at all times to avoid anyone seeing the fake thumb – really let go. But above all...

Practise Practise Practise!

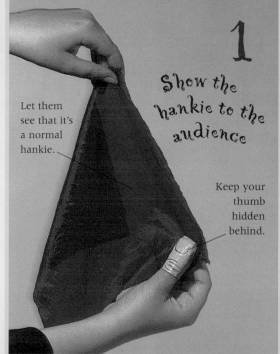

1

Show the hankie to the audience

Let them see that it's a normal hankie.

Keep your thumb hidden behind.

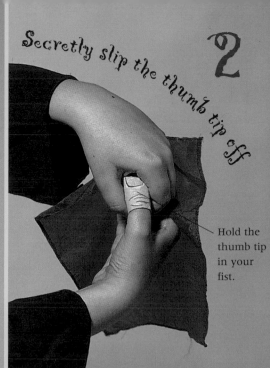

2

Secretly slip the thumb tip off

Hold the thumb tip in your fist.

3

Push the hankie into the tip

The audience will think that you are pushing it into your hand.

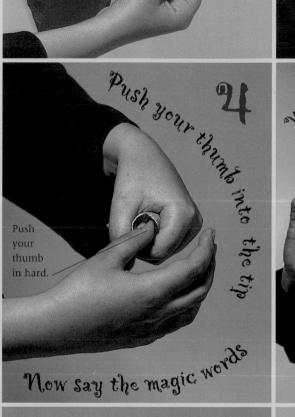

4

Push your thumb into the tip

Push your thumb in hard.

Now say the magic words

5

Where is the hankie? It's gone!

It's in the thumb tip.

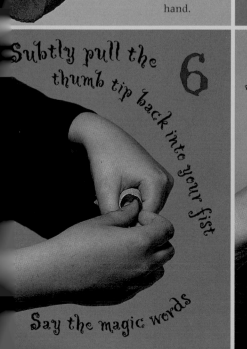

6

Subtly pull the thumb tip back into your fist

Say the magic words

7

Pull out the silk and slip the tip back onto your thumb

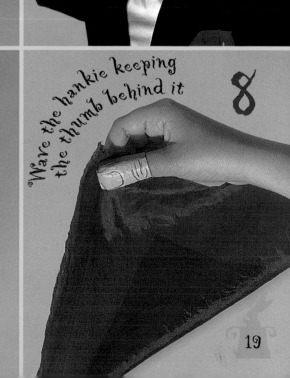

8

Wave the hankie keeping the thumb behind it

The Vanishing Coin

Who can lend me a coin? Assure the audience that they will see the money again as you make it disappear before their eyes. Then let them watch amazed as you magic it back!

Cylinder

See-through cup

Coin

Performing mat

Show the coin 1

Cover the cup 2

🐰 Magic it Back

Now that the coin has gone, perform the impossible and get it back. Mutter a few magic words, put the cylinder back on the cup, lift it up – and hey presto, the coin is back! Put the cylinder down, release it from the cup, and you have the same layout as the start. Give the coin back to the amazed owner.

Place the cylinder back over the cup and lift it up.

Don't let the cup slip out.

Phew it's back!

20

Prepare the Props

It is very important that your props all do their jobs well – they must be made very carefully. The performing mat and the cup base should be made from the same paper, the cup base must be fixed neatly, and the cylinder should exactly cover the cup – no bigger or smaller.

Performing mat

Be sure to make the mat big enough for the trick.

Cup cylinder

Cut the paper taller than the cup.

Tape it into a cylinder shape

Cut a strip of paper big enough to wrap around the cup.

Decorate the cylinder.

Cup base

Draw around the cup and cut the disc out.

Glue the paper disc to the rim of the cup.

Conceal the coin 3

Take off the cylinder It's GONE! 4

5 Performing the Trick

★ The key to this trick is that the base of the cup is covered with the same colour paper as the mat you perform your trick on.

★ Show everyone the cylinder and coin – but don't let anyone see the base of the cup. Then, follow the steps above to cover it all up.

★ Remember, the coin will always be under the cup but beneath the paper – so don't lift the cup up at all until you want to magic it back.

I can't believe my eyes

Where did my coin go?

Magic Wallet

Pop a note into the magic wallet and watch it evaporate into thin air by simply closing the wallet up and opening it again. Impossible!

Watch in wonder as things come and go from the magic wallet

In it goes

Pop the object inside the envelope

1

Bring it back

Fold the envelope up again

2

How to Make the Magic Wallet

This wallet is magical because it is back to front and front to back at the same time – whichever way you turn it.

Cut two pieces of thick card or cardboard, 21 x 15 cm (8 x 6 in).

Cut three 19 cm (7½ in) ribbons or strips of paper.

Cut the card and ribbons

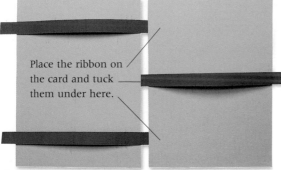

Place the ribbon on the card and tuck them under here.

Place the ribbon on the card

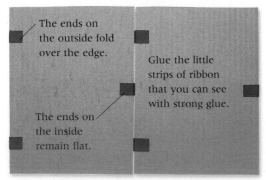

The ends on the outside fold over the edge.

Glue the little strips of ribbon that you can see with strong glue.

The ends on the inside remain flat.

Turn over the card. This will be the outside of the wallet.

Glue the ribbons in position

Take two identical envelopes.

Place one, with the opening facing down, underneath the ribbon

Get two identical envelopes

Glue the other envelope with the opening facing up exactly over the other one

Stick them under and over the ribbon

Glue some coloured paper to the outside of the wallet.

Cover up the outside

Make a design for both sides of the outside of the wallet, but make sure that they are exactly the same.

Decorate both sides the same

1 Follow this sequence

Try it out

Practise opening and closing the wallet both ways. It's amazing, isn't it? Once you have worked out how it works, you're ready to try it out.

The Secret?

The secret is that the wallet is double-sided. The way the ribbons are fixed makes it possible for you to open it two ways. Because of the way you have placed the envelopes, each has its own opening. So when you do the trick:

✳ Fill the envelope
✳ Close the wallet
✳ Open it the other way
✳ It's empty!

2 Open it up and pop in a star

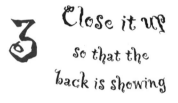

3 Close it up so that the back is showing

Open and close from left to right, just like this sequence, and you will see how it works.

4 Open it up the other way It's empty!

Remember it's front to back then back to front

5 Close it up again so that the front is showing again

Now you see how important it is that the front and back covers look the same.

6 Finally, open it up again and the star has returned

Miracle

Amaze your audience

by balancing your pet butterflies on the tips of pencils, straws, or even your nose. They float as if by MAGIC!

They can float anywhere – make lots and lots!

Attach weight here.

Use glue to stick a small coin to both wing tips.

🐰 Doing the Trick

To ensure that the audience is well and truly confused, hand everyone a butterfly without the weights attached. They'll be baffled when they can't balance it!

🐰 Fly Template

Use this outline to make your floating pet butterfly.

✱ Fold a piece of tracing paper in half and draw around the dotted line.

✱ Cut out this wing shape and open out the tracing paper.

✱ Trace the whole shape onto a piece of thin cereal packet card.

Use thin card, such as a cereal packet.

Make sure both sides are exactly the same

26

Cut out the shape

Butterflies

Don't tell anyone the secret!

Try it out on your fingertips

Colour it in   Glue on the weights

Bewildering Boxes!

Here are two empty boxes. Look, I can see right through them. Then, with the swish of a wand, a little magic happens.

Works like a charm!

I put one box over the other, say abracadabra, and out pops...

How is it done?

Take two boxes, one bigger than the other, and big enough for the boy to fit inside. Cut out the top and bottom of each box so that they can fold flat. The big box should fit over the smaller one. Decorate them.

To make the boxes taller, you can tape up the flaps.

Cut a secret door in the small box

Squash them flat and rest them against a chair.

Wand

Magic cloth

Big box

The secret door is hidden at the back.

2 Look, here is an empty box

Place the small box in front of the big box, with the secret door at the back.

Your amazing appearing boy must sit very quietly – no-one must know he is there.

3 Here is the other box – see, it's empty too

Now put the large box over the small box. If no-one has seen the boy, your trick is going well.

A Bird's Eye View
Here's what the audience can't see.

Shhh! I'm hiding behind the boxes

The small box must be at the edge of the big one so that the boy is still hidden.

Now I will crawl inside the box very carefully and very quietly

Hello up there!

Now I wait for the magic words — then I'll jump up

4 Wham bam alacazam!

Place the magic cloth over the box.

Whisk off the magic cloth.

Surprise!

At the end of the trick, fold up the boxes so that they are flat again.

Mind Power

Come and see Gypsy Rose and hear what she has to say. But watch out, she may know a bit more than you would like her to!

I know what you'r thinking, you think I can't read min Is that right?

Master the power of suggestion

The secret o mind-readin

The secret of mind power is that no-one, n even Gypsy Rose, can actually read minds. B there are many tricks that you can use to ma people believe that you can. Here are a few way

Picture Prediction

Guess right every time with this trick. Ask someone to pick a card. Tell them that you knew that they would pick that card and prove it by showing them the one in the envelope.

Inside this envelope is your prediction

1

2

Ask the volunteer to think hard before picking one of your cards.

Pick a picture
Are you sure you want the car?

They can change their mind but must settle on a definite one in the end.

3

Dramatically pull out the envelope with the right card in it.

Don't let anyone see inside the envelopes.

Amazing! My prediction was right
I knew you would pick the car

Setting up the Trick

The large envelope contains two others and each one holds a card. All you have to do is remember which envelope they are in.

Draw two sets of pictures

One picture should go in each envelope.

Put the small envelope into the middle sized one and pop the middle sized one into the large one.

Seal in the predictions

Pull out the envelope containing the chosen card

Mind-Reading Miracles

These mind power tricks will need the help of a glamorous assistant. Choose carefully, however, you need someone you can trust with all your secrets.

Black Magic

Gather a group of friends together and then you leave the room.

✳ Your assistant asks someone to pick any object in the room.

✳ When you return, your assistant asks you "is it the window?" "Is it the...?"

✳ To all the answers you say, "no", until you hear the word black. You then know that the next object will be the one. "Is it the black pen?" "No"

✳ "Is it the crystal ball?" "Yes!"

This or That?

Here's another way to do the trick.

✳ Ask the group to choose another object while you are out of the room.

✳ When you return your assistant asks you "Is it this cup? Is it this pen? Is it this cat?" To which you answer "no".

✳ But when he says the question "Is it THAT ball?" You say "Yes".

✳ When your assistant says the word "that", it's the right object.

A Feel for the Answer

Draw a circle with numbers on it, as below. Mark it from one to six, and place an object on each one. Get a group together.

✳ Ask someone to choose one of the objects in the circle and whisper what it is to your assistant, without you overhearing.

✳ Now you will read your assistant's mind, by simply touching his head, and tell the group what the object was.

✳ Put your hands on the side of his face. When the assistant squeezes his back teeth, you can feel it. The assistant will clench the number that the object is on.

The group chooses the bottle

Now for the mind power

The bottle is on the number three.

The assistant remembers the number.

Ah yes, I'm feeling the vibes It's the bottle!

The assistant squeezes his back teeth together three times and now you know that it is the bottle.

Works Like a Charm!

Lay out nine charms – in three rows of three. They can be anything you like, toys, books, even people.

✳ Ask your group to choose a charm when you leave the room.
✳ When you return, you will tell them which one they chose. How? By reading their minds, of course!

This is the one you all picked

Wow! You must have read our minds

The Secret is Your Trusty Assistant

Your assistant is with the group when the object is chosen, but nobody knows who she really is. She cunningly pretends that she is part of them and acts just as surprised when you guess right.

✳ When you go back into the room, your assistant lets you know which object has been chosen by touching a certain part of her body.
✳ Before the trick, you will have worked out a code so that each item is represented by a part of her body.

✳ IT'S SO EASY!

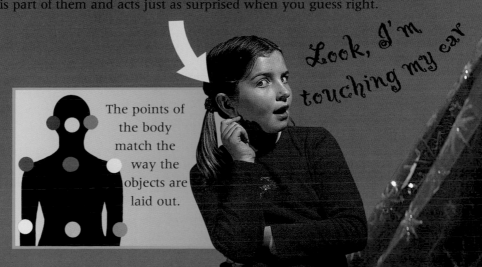

The points of the body match the way the objects are laid out.

Look, I'm touching my ear

Mathemagic

Even if you hate maths, you can still be a mathemagician. It's easy – all you have to do is follow the rules and the clever bit is done for you.

Pick any number from a star

Which stars do you see it on?

The person says their number is on red and green. That's 8+2=10.

If it's on red and green...

...then your number is 10

Pick a number

* Draw four star cards, exactly the same as the big ones on the left. The numbers must be in the same places.
* The key numbers are the ones in the middle of each star – 1, 2, 4, and 8.
* Ask someone to pick a number and then tell you which stars it appears on.
* All you do then is add up the numbers in the middle of the chosen stars and that will tell you what their number is

These are the magic numbers

Alternatively

If you are really clever, remember which numbers are in the middle of each star and perform the trick without even looking at them! Blue = 1, Red = 2, Yellow = 4, Green = 8.

4 2 8 6 5 4 7 3 1

By the power of the balloon, I will predict the answer

9
Don't let anyone see the magic number.

645
456 -
189
1 + 8 + 9 = 18
1 + 8 = 9

★ Write the number 9 on a piece of paper, slip it inside the balloon, and blow the balloon up.

★ Ask someone to pick a three digit number.

★ Jumble up the three numbers in any way to make another number.

★ Take the smaller number away from the larger one.

★ Add the digits in the answer together.

★ If they equal more than one digit, ie. a number over nine, keep adding them together until you have one number.

The answer will always be 9

Show everyone that you are putting your prediction into the balloon.

The number chosen is 645. Jumble the numbers in any way and you get 456. 645 - 456 = 189.

Add the 1, 8, and 9 and you get 18. Add the 1 and the 8 and you get the magic number 9.

Pop!

9

Alternatively

Try a very big number like 4,672,953 and jumble it up in the same way, taking the smaller one away from the larger one. The answer will still be 9. I promise!

It's unbelievable, the prediction is correct!

37

Hissing Spells and Powerful Potions

Stir up a brew of fizzing, bubbling concoctions and cast a spell from your enchanted charm book that's invisible to mere mortals and for a wizard's eyes only.

Wizards everywhere let's get busy

Mix up some potions and keep the secret recipes tied up in your magic book

Hubble, bubble, fizzle and bang,
A lizard's tail and a vampire's fang

What makes a Powerful Potion?

Believe it or not, there are magic ingredients in your very own kitchen. You just need to know which ones to mix together to get the explosive results!

Salt

Bicarbonate of soda

❦ Ingredients

All of the ingredients are quite safe but most of the mixtures taste really yucky. So don't drink them unless you are told you can.

Vinegar

Food colouring   Ice cream

Fizzy drink

Croak Croak

Bubble & Fizz

For an instant fizz, simply fill a small glass with any kind of fizzy drink you like. Then all you have to do is pour a teaspoon of salt on top. Add some food colouring for multi-coloured bubbles.

Pour salt into the drink

Watch it fizz up right over the top

Instant Inflation

Amaze your audience by telling them that you will blow up a balloon without blowing at all.

Don't let the soda out yet!

Pick up the balloon and empty out the bicarbonate of soda.

First pour some vinegar into a bottle.

Then pour a teaspoon of bicarbonate of soda into a balloon and stretch it over the top.

Add the secret ingredient

As the bicarbonate of soda mixes with the vinegar it bubbles up and forces air into the balloon, which makes it blow up all by itself. Let's hope it doesn't explode as well!

Release the magic

It has blown up by itself no-one has touched it

Look! It's still growing When will it stop?

Powerful Punch

Now this is a magic potion that you can drink – and it's yummy! Pour out a glass of any fizzy drink and fill it to the top. Then all you do is make sure that your friends are watching and add in a scoop of ice cream. The effects and the taste are sensational!

Pour out a fizzy drink

Add some ice cream

A frenzy of froth and foam

Take a sip while it froths I dare you!

Hubble Bubble

For some serious bubbles try this powerful potion – but don't drink it! Half fill a bottle with vinegar and drop in a teaspoon of bicarbonate of soda. If you want some longer-lasting froth then add a little washing-up liquid to the vinegar!

Bicarbonate of soda

Vinegar and washing-up liquid mixture.

Stand back! The bubbles keep on growing!

Hubble Bubble Trouble

47

To make a Magic Book

Keep your tricks and spells safe and sound in your very own magic book. Take two pieces of cardboard and some paper, punch two holes down one side of them, and tie them together with a ribbon.

Invisible Ink

Use this invisible ink to write secret spells in your book, or to send messages to other wizards.

Write with the magic ink

Lemon juice is the magic ink

You'll need to remember what you have written, because you can't see it!

How it's done
* Take a piece of paper – cheap colouring paper is best.
* Write your secret message on the paper in lemon juice with a paintbrush.
* To decipher the message, ask someone to iron the paper with a hot iron until the message comes through.

Ask an adult ...
to help you with the iron – it gets hot!

Tear the edges of the paper for an aged effect.

Stick your spells into your magic book.

Hocus Pocus

these magic messages will remain invisible to all non-wizards

Quick Tricks

As a magician it's always useful for you to keep a few nifty, quick tricks up your sleeve. Polish up your act and impress anyone anywhere. Try some of these out.

Watch out!

It really is a magic wand!

Practise your performance in front of a mirror and you'll leave your audience open-mouthed!

Wow, the wand is floating!

It's astonishing, how do you do it?

Magic Wand

This trick is great for the beginning a show. Simply grip the wrist of the hand supposedly holding the wand while actually holding it with the index finger of the gripping hand. Don't let anyone see how you do it

Link-up Trick

This trick is so cunning that how it works is a mystery. But who cares, the fact is it does! Follow the instructions and pull – that's magic!

Fold the piece of ribbon in two ways, as shown here.

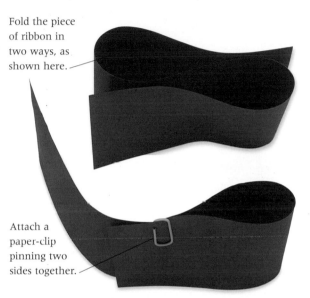

Attach a paper-clip pinning two sides together.

Add another paper clip attaching the other two sides, as shown.

Pull

Pull

Now, hold the two ends on either side and pull quickly.

It's a miracle! They are joined together.

Box Clever

You'll need to be slick at this trick to make it work. Before you start, plant a coin in your pocket, or even someone else's, that is the same as the one that you put in the box. You'll see why.

Pop a coin into a box

Shake it around and let it rattle. Making sure no-one can see what you are doing, turn it upside down, squeeze the sides, and let the coin slip out into your hand.

It's astonishing, the coin has gone Where can it be?

Now retrieve the other coin from your pocket or if you have managed to plant one on someone else, ask that person to look in their pocket. The magic coin has switched places!

Here's the card

Now it will disappear with the flick of a hand.

Now you see it

Now you don't. Show the card to the audience and in a blink of an eye it has vanished. Then bring it back again.

🐰 But How?

Cover the back of the card with black paper and perform the trick against a black background. Practise flipping it so that it disappears completely.

Where has it gone?

Keep this trick quick. Do it then get straight on with the next one.

Card in a Glass

Pick a card from a pack, then watch it go into the glass and disappear without a trace. How is it done? With a fake card, of course!

Show off the cards

Cover the cards with a hankie and pull out the fake card. Put the cards down.

Push the fake card into the glass.

See the shape of the card beneath

Ta daaa

Leave the fake card in the glass and pull hankie away.

The card has gone!

The glass looks empty.

🐰 What's the fake card?

The fake card is actually see-through plastic, which you must cut to exactly the same size as a card. Hide it behind the pack and make sure you pick it from underneath the hankie. In the glass it disappears!

Bottoms Up

Set up the cups in a row and announce that by turning only two cups at a time, and always ones next to each other, you will succeed in getting them all bottoms up. Then, challenge someone else to do it - and they can't!

First set them up like this

Turn over cups 1 and 2.

Remember this is your turn

Turn over cups 2 and 3.

They are now bottoms up

Now, challenge the other person

But for them set the cups up like this

Now let them try. And no matter how many times they turn two cups at a time, they will never get all their bottoms up. Remember to set them up this way for them.

Lost for Magic Words?

Try these out

* Abracadabra * Alacazam
* Hocus Pocus * Hey Presto!
* Izzy wizzy, wand get busy

Open sesame!

Remember the Magician's Code

* Don't give the secret away
* Never repeat your tricks

INDEX

Ace 44
Assistant 34, 35

Baffling balloon 10-13
Bag 4, 6, 8, 9
Bag of tricks 6-9
Balloon 10, 11, 12, 13, 37, 41
Bewildering boxes 28-31
Bicarbonate of soda 40, 41, 42
Black Magic 34
Box 28, 29, 30, 31, 45
Brew 38
Bubble 41, 42
Butterfly 26, 27

Car 8, 33
Cards (pack of) 44, 46
Charm 35, 38
Cocktail stick 12
Coin 20, 21, 26, 45
Crystal ball 34

Envelope 22, 24, 25, 33

Fake card 46
Fingertips 27
Fizzy drink 40, 41, 42
Floating wands 14-15
Food colouring 40, 41

Gypsy Rose 32

Handkerchief 6, 8, 9, 16-19

Ice cream 40, 42
Illusion 17
Ingredients 40, 41
Invisible ink 43

Jack-in-the-box 29

Magic book 39, 43
Magic cloth 30, 31
Magic potion 42
Magic wallet 22-25
Magician 4, 5, 14, 44
Magician's code 5, 47
Mathemagic 36-37
Mathemagician 36
Mind power 32-35
Miracle butterflies 26-27

Performing mat 20, 21
Picture prediction 33
Potion 38, 39, 40, 42
Powerful punch 42
Prediction 33, 37
Prop 5

Quick tricks 44-47

Recipe 39
Ribbon 24, 25, 43, 45

Salt 40, 41
Secret 5, 8, 9, 12, 13, 14, 15, 18, 25, 27, 30, 32, 34, 35, 39, 41, 43, 47

Secret message 43
Show 4, 5
Skewer 12, 13
Spell 38, 43
Star 36
Stick 11, 12, 13
Straw 26

Thumb tip 18, 19

Vanishing coin 20-21
Vinegar 40, 41, 42

Wallet 22, 23, 24, 25
Wand 14, 15, 28, 44
Wizard 4, 18, 38, 43

ACKNOWLEDGEMENTS

With thanks to . . .
Maisie Armah, Charlotte Bull, Billy Bull, James Bull,
Sophie Jones, Sorcha Lyons, and Kristian Revelle for being
model magicians

All images © Dorling Kindersley.
For further information see: www.dkimages.com